DOGHOUSE
SURVIVAL
GUIDE
FOR MEN

30 Scenarios and
30 Ways to Suck Up

This book is an original publication of Survivin' The Doghouse, LLC.

Survivin' The Doghouse
Survival Guide
30 Scenarios & 30 Ways to Suck up
Witten by Leora Burnet, Noel Wilkins and Earl McCall

For information contact:
Survivin' The Doghouse
111 Woodlyn
Willow Grove PA 19090
Info@survivinthedoghouse.com

Survivin' The Doghouse, LLC web address:
www.survivinthedoghouse.com

Printed in the United States of America

ISBN 978-0-578-11236-7

ACKNOWLEDGMENTS

First and foremost, writing this guide was a fun-filled adventure. And as with most adventures, there is a whole cast of people who contributed along the way. From the very start, this guide would not have been created if not for a friend's pending marriage, which planted the seed we used to create the entire doghouse idea. First, let us begin by thanking Steve Hyams for announcing his engagement and allowing us to poke fun at his future doghouse stays!

Most importantly, a heartfelt thanks goes out to our wives Liz, Leigh and our children Kaylee, Madison, and Mason. For without their support and sacrifice, this guide would not have been possible. They adjusted their schedules to give us the time needed for those long hours we spent isolated on our computers during the creation of this guide. We love you guys!

We would also like to thank Leora Burnett, one of our talented creative writers. We challenged her with numerous crazy scenarios as to why men end up in the doghouse accompanied by men's crazy excuses for acting the way we do. Leora was tasked with creating the feminine response to these outrageous situations, in turn helping men better understand where they went wrong. Her witty, humorous and sincere replies to each scenario, really showcases her talent! Without her, this guide would not have met our expectations. An amazing job Leora!

In addition to these, we want to thank Eleni Valasis who also contributed as creative writer and editor. She was instrumental in adding a different creative perspective to the design and wording to some of the scenarios. She made sure our guide design was right on point, mistake free, and a joy to read. Many thanks Eleni!

A special thanks to Chris Pawlowski, for her allowing us yet another set of editing skills. Her contribution aided all of us in the many changes needed to bring this amazing guide to publication!

Hats off to our very talented artist Egle Baksaite who provided the illustrations, which really brings our concepts to life, as well as making the guide much more attractive. Well done, Egle!

Last but not least, to all of those who we have not named but have encouraged us with tremendous support to keep striving and to those who have passed on and are cheering for us from beyond: Know that we sincerely thank you and feel blessed that you are a part of this adventure.

Sincerely,
Noel and Earl

TABLE OF CONTENTS

PREFACE

Surviving' the Doghouse started as a little joke between some friends and quickly turned into something much bigger. Almost as soon as we started talking about it, we realized that the concept of being "in the doghouse" was something that absolutely ANY man in ANY relationship could relate to. After all, admit it, guys, we can be idiots when it comes to stepping up in a relationship. It just can't be helped—at least not until now.

Another thing we quickly realized was how much we had to say on the topic—A LOT! And that is due to personal experience on both of our parts. Certainly not boasting, but humorously admitting, we both have spent literally decades in the doghouse for every and any reason. That's where this guide came in. We saw that we actually (for once, according to our wives) had something constructive to add to a conversation.

Through our years in the trenches, we have discovered some valuable lessons; and, we've shared them all here with you. While we are by no means relationship counselors, we hope that some of our experiences will provide you with fun yet thought-provoking ways to look at the various relationship scenarios in which we all find ourselves from time to time, and to be honest, sometimes, too many times.

What's at the core of *Survivin' the Doghouse*? First and foremost, fun! We have found that laughing, communicating, and making an effort to find things to laugh about together are significant keys to sustaining and building a successful relationship. We think that all of

these ingredients can be found in this guide…
and so much more! Yes, sometimes it takes work,
but pay attention to what makes your partner
laugh, and then share things with her that you
find throughout the day that you just know
will make her laugh, even if it isn't so funny to
you. If it's something you know she will love,
send it. You can find articles, email jokes, funny
pictures or whatever. Let her know that she's
on your mind. How cool is it when you know
that someone knows exactly how to make you
laugh and smile even when you're not in the
mood?

Our goal in writing this guide was not only to
present hilarious scenarios to help you and your
buddies get some good laughs by busting on
one another to no end; but, to also give you a
fun and practical tool to share with your mate.
Going over these " suck up" scenarios together
will help break the ice on some uncomfortable

but commonly experienced relationship issues, and will help open a way for playful and sincere discussion.

It is our hope that this survival guide will leave you with a deep realization that relationships are about give and take, consideration, and respect. We so often get wrapped up in our own desires that we forget to consider what we have committed to in our relationships—making sure our partner can also find in us their greatest friend and lover, and, of course, vice versa!

You'll see a lot of scenarios in this guide that you can relate to and that you had probably had little understanding of as a dude until now. We walk you through the solutions you need, and give you a little dose of laughter along the way. We hope you get a kick out of this and enjoy the humor, but that you also see the value here as well. We believe in relationships and hope that, in some small way, this guide can help you and yours gain some humor and perspective in yours.

So, to our Doghouse brothers, stay strong! And to the ladies out there, know there's hope! Most of all, enjoy the read.

Earl, Noel

NAVIGATING YOUR SOCIAL LIFE

Whether you just started dating your girl or have been married to her for 20 years, it's pretty much guaranteed that at some point in the near future you are going to mess up big time in a social situation. It's inevitable, and you know it. The following scenarios will walk you through just what to do the next time you're out with your lady and stick your foot in it.

Doghouse Scenario #1 - The first date overshare

The Situation: You're sitting across the table from the most amazing girl you've ever seen in your entire life. Just when you think you've won

1

her over, you open your mouth and tell her one of your deepest, darkest secrets. The problem is that she was clearly not prepared to deal with the information you've just dropped on her plate. Whether you just told her you just got out of a short-term prison sentence for accidental vehicular homicide or you've professed your secret lust for feet, you are completely guilty of a first date overshare.

The Excuse: "Sorry, I just... I feel so comfortable around you, and you seemed so into me..."

Getting Out of the Doghouse: Let's face it, gentlemen... overshares are rarely comfortable, first date or not. Women are just as guilty of them, but women try to be very careful about what they share on a first date. They are always on their best behavior, and are also investigating to see if you are, too. The trick with this one, unfortunately, is prevention.

If you think it might help, sit down with yourself before a date and come up with a list of questions to ask her. Keep her talking about herself, and it will help you avoid the overshare. People love being asked questions, women especially, so if you are genuinely interested in who she is, what she likes, and what her goals are, you can easily avoid tasting your own foot.

DOGHOUSE SCENARIO #2 - The people pleaser

The Situation: The first few dates, you keep asking her to guide your adventures. "What would you like to do now?" "Where would you like to go?" "Is that okay?" "Did you have fun?" Your brain is all over the place trying to please her, but the problem is that you're showing her that your tiny male mind is incapable of forming thoughts and opinions of your own. No bueno.

The Excuse: "All I want to do is make you happy! It's my greatest goal in life, actually."

Getting Out of the Doghouse: She's on to you. She is well aware that you are not necessarily the most creative of creatures. Your "special friend" realizes that you may not have good ideas for your dates, but she expects you to try anyway. And yes, she realizes that's a little unfair.

The thing is, guys, there are tons of books, websites, and other resources with helpful, creative ideas to make each date different and awesome. If you're at a loss, or you're not very good at planning, there is help out there! The problem with letting her pick everything is this—while it seems like a really good idea at first, she's going to lose interest in you fast. Why? Because contrary to popular belief, women don't actually like to control everything all the time.* They like feeling like you put some thought behind your date because you like her enough to do so. Date nights are important, and they establish the mood for the rest of your relationship, which could turn out being a really long time, if you play your cards right!

DOGHOUSE SCENARIO #3 -
Bringing up personal issues when her friends are around

The Situation: You've been having a few drinks, and out of nowhere you decide to start talking about the four strangely shaped moles on her butt in front of her friends. Then when she gets mad, you decide to tone it down and talk about nice things like all the times she peed on herself from laughing too hard.

---

* This is *gold*. Seriously, save it for future use.

The Excuse: "I thought you said you weren't afraid to share anything with your friends!"

Getting Out of the Doghouse: Oh boy. We cannot actually express how badly you have kicked the dog with this one. Now, it should be noted that women screw up like this sometimes, right down to outing a guy's *exact* size to their girlfriends. Drinks can loosen the tongue to a rather uncomfortable level, and there really is no way around it. Things are going to get said that you will regret, come morning. The good news is that if they're good friends of hers, they probably already know darker secrets than you could ever tell them. The bad news? She's still utterly mortified.

The bare-bones issue here is that you've truly embarrassed her. You put her in an awkward position wherein she would usually feel *perfectly* comfortable. Essentially you have now created a scenario for her just like those dreams where you're giving a speech naked in front of a crowd. *Oops.* Depending on how sensitive your girl is, she may not ever get over the emotional scar of you making her friends laugh at her. The best thing you can really do is offer a sincere apology, once you're sober that is. Explain that you had no intention of hurting her, and you're ashamed you outed her personal stuff. Then (and this is the tricky part, guys) NEVER EVER drink around her friends again, if you can't keep your mouth shut.

DOGHOUSE SCENARIO #4 -
Not being a gentleman in public

The Situation: The umbrella is too small and, even though it's pouring, you selfishly and intentionally let her get a little more wet while you hold the umbrella more over yourself than her. Or you're out at an elegant restaurant and you let out a disgusting belch. *Or,* immediately afterwards, you burst into raucous laughter, because you think it's funny.

The Excuse: "I thought you were into equal rights." Or "Come on, hon. It's only a natural body function. Relax."

Getting Out of the Doghouse: Being a gentleman *anywhere* is always appreciated. Contrary to what you may believe, women do not expect men to be gentle all the time. They know that it takes work for most guys to remember to do simple little things that would be construed as romantic or otherwise gentlemanly. Most women who are not insane will not expect you to be a gentleman twenty-four/seven. However, once in a while, it would be nice.

The most egregious* scenarios are obviously in public. If you are acting like a juvenile delinquent,

---

* This means you're in it deep, my friend.

chances are your gal will not want to be seen in public with you anymore. If you're worried about the rain, bring two umbrellas. If you have to belch, close your damn mouth! There's time enough for letting one rip when you're out with your buddies. They'll find it funny, she won't.

DOGHOUSE SCENARIO #5 -
Eyeballing another chick's butt

The Situation: You're strolling through the mall together when your gal stops into a certain lingerie shop to pick out a little something special for later. While standing behind your lady as she pays at the counter, you decide to become fixated on the awesome ass that the cashier has. Unfortunately, the mirrors on the wall behind the register have given your lady a perfect view of your perfect view while you stared for two full minutes, with drool leaking from your mouth like a St. Bernard with a bone.

The Excuse: "I was just comparing. Yours is *way* better."

Getting Out of the Doghouse: Flattery will get you... well, okay, not everywhere... but pretty far. If your girl catches you checking out another girl, and you're unlucky enough *not* to be dating the bi-sexual who was also checking out the other girl, chances are she's probably a little butthurt that you don't check *her* out that way. She probably instantly wandered mentally back to a time when you used to eyeball her, and has realized that you don't anymore. Therefore, by doing this little action you thought was innocent and unnoticed, you've damaged her self-confidence.

"Men will be men." Fellas, women get that. They know you're probably always looking at, or thinking about, other women. They just don't want to see it actively happening when you're supposed to be thinking about them. Shrug off your indiscretion, tell her with the utmost sincerity that you think she's the most beautiful woman in the world, and then hug her. The hug is the cure-all pill. Most of the time.

DOGHOUSE SCENARIO #6 -
Flirting with her girlfriends

The Situation: Your lady is having friends over for one of those... "parties." You know the kind. A woman who is invariably part of one of those pyramid companies invades your house, lays out an obscenely girly display of something (candles/cooking supplies/Tupperware, etc.), and then the other women come, fawn over said items and then buy them. You retreat to your man cave upon their arrival, wanting no part in such shenanigans. After a few cold ones, you wander upstairs and notice a few unfamiliar, attractive faces in the group. You immediately find reasons to hang around and stare, while cracking a few inappropriate jokes and continually asking the hotties if they need anything.

The Excuse: "I just wanted to make sure your shindig was going well, honey!"

Getting Out of the Doghouse: Women are not stupid, FYI. Your spouse can probably tell that you were utterly transfixed by the beauty of her friends. If she is still friends with them by the end of the party, she probably won't be for long. Women do not like feeling inferior... and they don't admit it that easily. If her friends had been ugly as a pack of trolls (no offense) she knows full well that you would not have emerged until the house was silent and empty. As it stands, you ventured up out of curiosity and lingered while drooling all down the front of your shirt.

Unfortunately, there's no real instant fix for this one. Pry the ol' foot out of your mouth and try not to do it again. Women don't mind the occasional eyeing of another girl, but if it's obvious that you're interested— especially in her friends— things are not going to end well for you. Women do not need help destroying the fragments of self-esteem they still have.

Reassure her that she is the only one for you, and swear that you didn't mean to be a creep. You might also think about having a guys' night the next time she has one of these parties.

Doghouse Scenario #7 - Forgetting to introduce her to friends in public

The Situation: You're invited to a work social event. As you walk in the door, you notice a group of your co-workers engaged in a conversation. You grab your lady's hand, navigate through the crowd, and join right in... never taking the time to introduce her. She stands there awkwardly for ten minutes while everyone else has a jolly old time. Bad enough, but the same thing happened at the mall the other day when you ran into friends. *They* actually had to ask "Oh, is this your girlfriend?"

The Excuse: "I thought you'd already met all my co-workers!"

Getting Out of the Doghouse: Tell your lady that you really are sorry. You genuinely got distracted by the conversation and you certainly never meant for her to be excluded. Remind her that you love her, and that she's not invisible, because she probably feels a bit like she is. This one is really an easy fix. Make sure that you introduce your girl to new people *as soon as possible!* That way she'll feel more at ease, and perhaps she'll even join in the conversation herself.

DOGHOUSE SCENARIO #8 -
**Leaving her alone at social events
or parties**

The Situation: Mutual friends invite you and your girl to a party. When you arrive, you stay close to her as you make your way around the room. After a few drinks, you've loosened up quite a bit, and you're feeling like the life of the party! You become Mr. Social... but you forgot one thing—your girl. You have no idea that she's sitting alone, *sober*, in the corner.

The Excuse: "Sorry, baby, I didn't see you, so I thought you'd found a crowd to hang out with!"

Getting Out of the Doghouse: Alright, we admit it: This one is as much her fault as it is yours.* When social events turn out differently than expected, your partner may be taken aback. Should this occur, do not be surprised if your girlwife finds it impossible to allow herself to get easily re-engaged towards having a good time, since she is busy being irritated by whatever didn't go her way.

------

* No, seriously.

The most important advice we can give you is to check in with your lady every so often. Make sure she's having a good time, and if she isn't, stick with her. Try to convince her to come have a few drinks and do the limbo with you. If she feels like you are helping to include her, she'll forget about the things that didn't go right and start having fun. Yup, it really is that simple.

NAVIGATING YOUR RELATIONSHIP

O ne of the most exciting spaces? Between you and your lady. One of the most dangerous spaces? Between you and your lady.

Sometimes it seems like your sorry butt can't even say one word without ending up in the doghouse. The following scenarios will get you through any and every idiotic personal statement or unintentional insult you throw your lady's way.

Doghouse Scenario #9 - Coming in late

The Situation: You promised to not come home late, but then decided you were having way too much fun with the boys and thought to yourself "I'm my own man! I do what I want!", then stayed another two hours without calling home.

The Excuse: "Wow, I had no idea my watch was three hours fast! How the hell did *that* happen??"

Getting Out of the Doghouse: Here's a very helpful hint, gentlemen: women worry a *lot*. If you promise them you won't be home late, and then blatantly disregard this little fact, they are likely to start worrying that you're dead in a ditch somewhere around 11:30 or midnight. Once 2:00am rolls around, they're hysterical. We are not claiming it's a rational way of thinking, but you might want to consider the fact that your woman might be sitting at home dialing 9-1-1 to inform the police that she believes you may be dead, kidnapped, or abducted by Martians.

If you don't want to go home, pick up the phone and call her. Yes, she'll be pissed (reasonably so, since you *did* promise), but she won't be in near hysterics thinking something terrible has happened to you. Be upfront, and honest. Explain to her that you're having a good time. That is, if you're too much of a jerk not to keep your promise. Generally, guys, if you're honest, a woman will be much more understanding. Just tell her that you'd like to stay out late every once in a while with your guy friends. If she's a rational human being, she'll get that. After all, everyone needs their time away.

DOGHOUSE SCENARIO #10 - Coming in smelling like perfume

The Situation: You were at the bar, when you honestly and unexpectedly ran into some women from work, hung out with them for a short time, hugged them good bye, and then headed straight home.

The Excuse: "She's just a friend, I swear. Not *even* a friend. I work with her! Honestly, I barely remember her name!"

Getting Out of the Doghouse: It's pretty reasonable to expect that any woman is going to feel a little threatened by her man smelling like unfamiliar perfume. Likewise, excuses are only going to make her feel like you're lying to her. Honestly, even telling the truth might make her feel that way. The key to getting out of this one is presentation. Explain your entire story, in full, right down to the hug. Make it sound as though it was absolutely no big deal, because if you're telling the truth then she'll see that in your story and hear it in your voice.*

DOGHOUSE SCENARIO #11 -
Coming in drunk

The Situation: Three of your friends have to carry you into the house at 3:00am after a night of partying, when you promised that you wouldn't come in drunk... again.

---

* We believe you, don't worry.

The Excuse: "We were celebrating, uh, Wednesday!"*

Getting Out of the Doghouse: Alright. You messed up. Let's not beat around the bush when we all know it's true. You made a promise that you knew you couldn't (wouldn't) keep, and now you've upset her again. Let's put aside the potential moral issues here (possibly driving home drunk, for example) and consider the facts. You promised you would not come home drunk, and you did. Not only that, but you got so *very* plastered that it took three of your buddies to support your bad habit. I sure hope you're going to clean the vomit out of the floorboard of Bill's car.

Seriously, though. Women *do* understand that sometimes things get wild and crazy. Most of

---

* Psst! Today is Saturday.

them have attended or been witness to at least one wild bachelorette party in their time. They know that letting loose and getting drunk can be a lot of fun.

The other side of the coin, however, is that women will rarely come staggering in drunk at three in the morning to her man who has been sitting up sick with worry and anger. Like we said before, the only real "solution" here is to keep your promise. If you cannot do that, don't promise it. Have a serious sit-down talk with her about the need to occasionally let loose and have a good time. Make promises you *can* keep (i.e., "I promise that if I drink too much, to be safe, I'll hand the car keys to a sober driver." and "I'll call to check in if I'm going to be late/drinking."). Doing such is not only the responsible thing to do, but it also works to keep your gal from feeling like you have no regard for her feelings. Women are sensitive creatures, and they will not step off the "conclusion" bridge so much as throw themselves face-first into the abyss below... from which there is no turning back.

DOGHOUSE SCENARIO #12 - Always complaining while she shops

The Situation: As you pull into the shopping mall parking lot, you are already saying "How long are we going to be here?" You came along because she asked you to. As you walk around, she stops and looks at every display window. You keep walking while she stops, to try and keep her moving, which works about as well as watering grass with turpentine. She has to yell at you to stop and come over for a look... Then you act disinterested and yes her to death. She gets the hint, and is now grouchy. Way to go.

The Excuse: "I have a headache."

Getting Out of the Doghouse: Women get it—you don't like to shop. They really do get the fact that it's not your thing, and in fact, most will admit that they like the fact that men are not shoppers. The mistake you made was going along to begin with. It is always smarter to tell her straight-up that you really aren't into shopping, but she's free to go anyway. If she doesn't want to go alone, then she might insist, and you should probably be willing to tag along... but only if she insists.

If she does insist, and you *do* go along, remember the very simple advice offered herein: *Everything* is fantastic. Yes, every single thing she stops to look at, everything she takes an interest in... is awesome. Why? Because she wants to feel like you're listening. She doesn't really give a crap about that polka-dotted dress. In fact, she'll probably forget it even exists in about five minutes. By pointing things out and sharing her interest, she's trying to find common ground. If you are disinterested, she takes it to mean you don't want to hear her talk at all, and her feelings will get hurt. Yes, we know, women are confusing.*

DOGHOUSE SCENARIO #13 -
Not letting her express her opinion

The Situation: You are out with friends enjoying a great dinner and good conversation. Only one problem; you seem to be the spokesperson for the both of you. As soon as your lady is asked a question or starts to express her opinion on a subject, you, being the genius you think you are, cut in mid-conversation and never let her finish. You constantly interrupt her… and apparently think you always have a better answer. Oops.

---

* This is something you should have learned to accept by now, guys.

The Excuse: "I was just making sure they knew that I agreed with you!"

Getting Out of the Doghouse: Being interrupted is never fun. It's worse when you feel as though someone really doesn't want you to speak or thinks you're incapable. Keep in mind there was a time when women weren't allowed to speak—they will always hold grudges about this sort of thing. If you continue to break in and inform the group at-large that your spouse doesn't care for the way health care laws are slated, she will remember every single time and hold them *all* against you. We're not saying it's right, but she'll probably do it.

So how do you handle it? Well, let the woman speak. Women understand that men get excited. Especially if the man happens to approve of and appreciate his woman's opinion and interests.

The woman whose man knows her well enough to answer for her is a lucky gal indeed, and they usually know it. That doesn't mean they *want* you to answer for them all the time, every time. So glance at her before you open your mouth. Give her a chance to shine.

If it's too late, and you've already stepped on her toes, apologize most sincerely in front of the group (if possible), and make some off-handed joke about eating your own foot. Let the party laugh it off, and then mind your manners. She'll appreciate it later. Especially when you give her a heartfelt apology in private later on.

Doghouse Scenario #14 - Missing important dates

The Situation: You get home from work and she has this look of anticipation on her face. You are puzzled. You ignore her and ask what's for dinner? She turns and retreats to the bedroom and slams the door. You follow, wondering what the hell is wrong with her.* You ask her, absolutely clueless of the reason behind her sudden mood shift. Then she reminds you it's her birthday and that look of anticipation was her expecting a gift. *Oops... Big OOPS.* Last time it was your anniversary. Now you're really in trouble.

The Excuse: "I'm so sorry, honey! They were out of (insert appropriate gift for your spouse, here) when I tried, so I had to order it, but it's on standby and they still haven't called me..."

Getting Out of the Doghouse: The "I ordered you a gift, it just hasn't arrived yet" excuse never ever works. Women are, in fact, smarter than a box of staples, and they are very much

---

* Don't even think about suggesting it's PMS. Don't even think it. Seriously. Are you crazy?

insulted when you imply they are not. Nine times out of ten, forgetting important events is probably one of the worst things you can do. Women aren't perfect about remembering things, either, but birthdays, anniversaries and Valentine's Day are usually a pretty big deal.

We advise you to get a calendar. You don't even have to pay for it. There are dozens of free calendars online. Get one, and fill in *all* of these super-important dates so this will *never* happen again. Then, kick yourself twenty times in the ass for being a shmuck (she'd never forget *your* birthday), take her out to dinner wherever she wants to go, and then drop by her favorite store for some quality shopping. It may not be the thoughtful birthday gift she was hoping for, but it will do in a pinch.

Make absolutely certain that you tell her how genuinely sorry you are that you forgot what day it was. Tell her the date slipped your mind, and that you wish you had planned better. Also, swear that it won't ever happen again... thanks to your new calendar.

Doghouse Scenario #15 - Spending too much time at work

The Situation: You work late, kissing up to the boss every chance you get. You can feel it... that promotion is just around the corner. You want that big office and all the perks that go along with it. One problem—you constantly lose track of the time and are frequently late getting home. Cold dinners, cold stares, and the silent treatment when you arrive home, even though you called and said you would be late! Time for a change.

The Excuse: "I just want to give you a better life."

Getting Out of the Doghouse: She gets it, dude. She wants you to get that promotion just as much as you do. The only problem is that you're having an affair with your job. It may not be a sexual affair, but you're spending more and more time there, sacrificing your home life so that you can be a better employee. Trust us, it doesn't have to be one or the other. A balance is not only doable, but healthy. Go in early rather than staying late, or if you must stay late, pick a *set* time that you will work until and stick to it. If she knows you're working until seven, she can put off dinner until you get home to eat it warm.

She wants to feel like she's important too. The promotion is a big deal. She understands that. She may be glaring across the table at you, but she absolutely supports you in your endeavors. The only trouble is that, despite her support, she feels like she's getting nothing for her efforts, and she's undoubtedly frustrated by that. Make time for her. Even if you get home late, finish dinner, ask if she wants to rent a movie, or even go out to one. Let her know that even though you're working hard, you love her more than anything in the world.

Doghouse Scenario #16 - Not calling her all day while you are at work

The Situation: You're busy, busy, busy 8 hours a day at work. You seem to forget that other things exist outside of the office during those long days. You always have this nagging feeling during work that you forgot something. You are reminded as you arrive home that you DO have a life outside of work and that your lady does actually exist.

The Excuse: "I'm sorry. I forgot you were so needy."

Getting Out of the Doghouse: No, seriously. If your woman is really that unhappy that you don't call her every day while you're at work, it's time to have a serious talk. We know all the ways guys can screw up, but this (surprisingly) isn't really one of them. Women... most women... realize that work gets crazy. There's not always time to call and check in, and really, why would they expect that? It's a work day! If your woman is the type who really does like talking to you at work, make time to give her a call on your lunch break. If that isn't good enough, sit down with her and have a discussion about why she feels the need to talk to you while you're working. Don't be tactless, but express your concern that she might be just a hair self-conscious.

Doghouse Scenario #17 -
Not noticing her changing appearance, hair, makeup, etc.

The Situation: She tells you this weekend she is going to get her hair styled and colored. You half hear her and say "That's great, dear". She arrives home later that day and you are glued to the TV. As she enters the room with her newly styled hair, you look up and politely ask if she can grab you a beer. She returns and throws it in your direction, reminding you she has just returned from the salon. You finally look up and lo and behold... she does look different! Her hair has changed color. Too late! You missed your cue!

The Excuse: "I didn't think you wanted me to make a big deal out of it. You *did* mention you were going, after all! It wasn't a surprise or anything!"

Getting Out of the Doghouse: Alright, yes, women can be a little bit sensitive about that sort of thing.* They like to feel like you're going to notice every little change they make, and the truth is... you usually don't. Honestly, gentlemen, women are a little crazy about their appearance sometimes. Really, though, they don't expect you to notice every change, but if she specifically mentions that she's going to have her hair done and then you *don't* take notice, that is completely and totally your fault.

The best way to get out of this one on an immediate level is to pretend you were just kidding about not noticing. Tell her the honest truth about her new do (whether you like it or not, just remember to utilize tact if you don't), and apologize for not saying something when she got home.

---

* Yes, this means "overly sensitive".

37

Doghouse Scenario #18 - Not paying enough attention to your personal hygiene

The Situation: It's the weekend! No need to bathe, shave, wear clean clothes or use deodorant... because you ain't going anywhere. So you think to yourself, "Oh, what the hell?" This has become a weekly routine of yours, and it feels great. The problem is that you look and smell like a Sasquatch. She keeps her distance and reminds you she married a man and *not* an ape!

The Excuse: "But honey! It's manly. Don't you want me to feel manly?"

Getting Out of the Doghouse: We're going to say this as politely as possible... take a damn shower, dude. You reek like bad cheese and old socks, and that is *never ever* a good combo. Yes, it's the weekend, and yes, you have every right to kick back and relax after a hard week at work, but that's *no* reason not to start your day with a shower and clean clothing at the very least. You're not a teenager, anymore. You're a grown up. Act like one!

We can pretty much guarantee that it isn't just her that feels this way, by the way. This habit is a terrible habit, and you should be ashamed for indulging! We don't mean to berate you, but honestly, it's kind of hard to stand here talking to you. You really should go take that shower. *Now.*

Doghouse Scenario #19 - Not being romantic enough

The Situation: You have a routine, you go to work, come home, eat, have sex and go to sleep! You are a machine! Now therein lies the problem. You treat your lady as though she is also an android. Unbeknownst to you, she is a living, breathing bag of emotions that needs your constant snuggling, cuddling and attention to function.

The Excuse: "I thought you got over that 'romance' thing a long time ago? That stuff is so commercial, anyway."

Getting Out of the Doghouse: This one is a little bit tricky. Mainly because, by the time she notices you've stopped being romantic, you haven't done anything romantic in a really long time. And really, it's an understood thing that sometimes romance just... goes away. But that doesn't mean that it isn't nice to revive it every now and again.

The suggestions we offer are simple ones. Offer to go for a nice summer evening stroll with her. Maybe plan a picnic. Bringing home flowers is also a good one. The important thing to remember here is that women are fairly easy to please.* They do not require monumental efforts on your part to be impressed or pleased. Little gestures are just as appreciated, and in the end, they are the ones she'll think of first when she's recounting to her friends the hundred reasons why you're better than all the ones before.

---

* No, really. We mean it.

NAVIGATING
YOUR HOME

Your home is your castle? And every man knows that the lady is the one who sets the rules—and you better be playing by them. Violating the rules of your queen's kingdom is one of the best ways to get sent straight to the doghouse before you can even say *boo*. The following scenarios will get you through every missed chore and raised toilet seat.

DOGHOUSE SCENARIO #20 -
Not doing the dishes

The Situation: She kindly asks you to help out around the house by doing the dishes and you say, "Of course!" knowing full well that you had absolutely no intention of ever getting them done.

The Excuse: "See? This is exactly why you don't want me to do the dishes!"

Getting Out of the Doghouse: Honestly, humor might be your best way to get out of this one. Women love to smile. If you can smooth things over by making yourself look like an apologetic dolt, chances are she'll be much more willing to forgive your oversight. Say you're sorry, joke about what a punk you are, and then get the dishes done right away! And next time? Do what you said you would do… or don't promise it.

DOGHOUSE SCENARIO #21 -
Bleaching the color clothes

The Situation - You're watching the game and your significant other nags you to do the laundry. Out of frustration (or to shut her up), you reluctantly rush to the washer, carelessly throw in clothes, detergent and BLEACH— close the lid, start the machine, and rush back with the hope that you haven't missed anything. You congratulate yourself on being the ultimate house husband and think you've found the perfect game/chore balance. However, while you're really enjoying your game, her favorite "color" clothes are being miserably turned into horrible colors.

The Excuse: "Well, hey, you needed new clothes anyway!"

Getting Out of the Doghouse: It's time for a shopping spree. No, really. Women understand that men are only human, but they are always somewhat less than amused when their men accidentally destroy things— especially clothes. Clothes are a sacred thing, for most gals. If you have truly destroyed an entire load of her favorite things, you need to do everything you can to make amends. If that means dropping a good couple hundred out of your savings, then you had better do it with a smile on your face. Yes, it sucks, but hey... that's what you get for putting bleach in with color clothes.

Doghouse Scenario #22 - Not making requested repairs

The Situation: She asks you for the past two weeks to make a simple repair and you intentionally procrastinate, knowing full well it will catch up to you.

The Excuse: "Sorry, honey. I totally forgot! I'll get to it soon.*

Getting Out of the Doghouse: Let's be honest. You didn't forget. And you probably don't have any real intention of getting to it soon. The above apology usually only means something if it's followed up with action. Women know full well that men are just as bad at procrastinating as they are. They are also not as dumb as some men think they are. Women know you're putting them off. And, guys, putting them off is probably your worst idea *ever*. The problem with broken things (whether it's a small hole in the wall, a broken lawn mower, or a busted lamp) is that they bring down the general integrity of your environment. If you have things that need to be fixed, not fixing them is like not bathing. Eventually, it just stinks.

---

* This is what you said the last seven times she asked.

It's important to realize that you should stop procrastinating not for her sake, but for your own! If it can't be fixed, get rid of it and get a new one, but take the steps to make it right. Putting her off only makes you look like a total shmuck. If you walked into someone's house and there was a hole in the wall, or a broken toilet, wouldn't you feel a little like maybe that person lived in a crappy place? Yeah, me too. *Fix it.*

Doghouse Scenario #23 - Not taking out the trash and missing the trash truck

The Situation: She's been reminding you since the close of dinner last night to put the trash out, but you insisted on waiting until the morning... and *overslept.*

The Excuse: "You know, I chased the trash truck halfway down the block and he flipped me off! Jerk! I'll get it out next week, for sure."

Getting Out of the Doghouse: Unfortunately, guys, she's probably just going to be mad at you for this one. Short of loading up all that smelly garbage into your shiny new car and driving it to the dump, you pretty much have no choice but to see proof of your transgression sitting in your garage for a week. Maybe your guilt will remind you not to procrastinate. We know it probably won't. Your best solution in this circumstance is to take care of things *immediately* when she asks. Yes, we know that you want to relax in front of the television. Women support you in this. And maybe, just maybe, your partner would join you in devising a streamlined taking-the-trash-to-the-curb plan that could reduce your mandated trash removal process down to five minutes. Ask her! The least she could do is say no.

Doghouse Scenario #24 -
Not helping with grocery bags

The Situation: She got up early to run some important errands, and then went food shopping. You sat around in your pajamas all morning, until you saw her pull into the driveway with *a lot* of bags in the car... so you hightailed it into the shower.

The Excuse: "I'm so sorry, honey, I was in the shower."

Getting Out of the Doghouse: You're lame. You're also a little bit of a jerk. The worst part is, you know it. The bad part is that your poor, unsuspecting spouse probably has no idea. She's probably a little miffed that she had to carry everything in by herself, but she figures it's a coincidence that you just *happened* to be in the shower when she got home. She accepts your apology at face-value because she doesn't know you were peeking through the curtains like a demented neighbor when she unsuspectingly pulled into the driveway with her load of heavy bags.

The only solution is to help her.* Smart guys will carry the groceries and let the woman do the unpacking/putting away. Think of it this way; unloading takes less time, and she'll *still* be grateful, because she'd rather be putting things away than carrying those heavy bags.

DOGHOUSE SCENARIO #25 -
Forgetting to pick up an item you were asked to get on the way home

The Situation: You are be-boppin' along the highway chillin' to some of your favorite tunes when your cell phone rings. It's your girl calling

---

* Mind-blowing, we know.

to ask you to grab a few items on your way home. No problem, right? Upon your arrival home, she discovers half the items that she requested are missing. It wouldn't be so bad... except last time you forgot to stop at all.

The Excuse: "They were out of almost *every-thing!* I guess there was some sort of flash flood panic."

Getting Out of the Doghouse: Get back in the car with your tail between your legs and go right back to the store with a *written* list this time. She'll probably insist that you don't *have to*... but you really do. You know you do. And while you're at the store, grab something nice for her. A new movie, a book... whatever you think she might like. It will make her smile to know that not only were you willing to fix your mistake immediately, but you also know how to kiss just enough ass to show her you know you're sorry.

DOGHOUSE SCENARIO #26 -
Leaving articles of clothing lying around

The Situation: You get home from work and your ladys not home yet, so you decide to check out what's on the sports channel. You kick off your shoes, throw off your sports coat, and grab a beer. A few minutes later it's break time, so you head upstairs to the bathroom. She arrives home and notices your attire clinging to various pieces of furniture. Last time, it was the bedroom.

The Excuse: "Huh? The dog must have dragged them out."*

Getting Out of the Doghouse: First, clean up your stuff. It will soften her temper drastically if she doesn't have to chew your butt more than once. Second, learn a very important lesson—she's angry because she feels you do

* Do you actually own a dog?

not respect her or the home you share together. It's perfectly acceptable to steal some time with your television and the sports channel, but steal some time with your other household items first (like the closet). The long and short of it is this: It's a matter of respect. Respect your spouse, and respect the space you share with her. You will hardly ever catch a woman leaving her clothing willy-nilly around the house. Now, of course we admit there are exceptions to that (there always are), but that doesn't mean you should fall behind.

DOGHOUSE SCENARIO #27 -
Not cleaning up after having friends over

The Situation: You promise that, when your friends left, you'll clean up, since (surprise!) you forgot the last time. This time you party hard through two football games with the works: chips, dip, beer, pretzels, etc. As your buds leave they say, "Hey man, you need help cleaning up this crap?" You decline in a manly fashion, "Nah I got it... don't worry about it." Then, you retreat upstairs, lose track of time, and come down 30 minutes later to see the her cleaning up your waste! It worked last time...

The Excuse: "They promised they'd help me clean up, and then they *bailed* on me! Those jerks!"

Getting Out of the Doghouse: Let's face it, gents. Blaming it on your friends rarely (if ever) works. Seriously, women can tell when you're handing them a handful of bull and calling it chocolate. If she comes in to find that your shared space is disheveled because you and your friends* made a huge mess, she's going to be pissed anyway.

---

* Face it. They're manlier than you because at least they offered to help.

The best thing to do, if caught in the act of *not* cleaning up, is to immediately apologize for not getting to it already, and start helping her clean up. If she sees you jumping to and cleaning up something you should have already taken care of, it will soften her. Then, she switches from being pissed because she's cleaning it up alone to being happy that you are helping out. It's a dirty trick, but it totally works.

DO NOT procrastinate cleaning up or leaving her to start the tidying up routine all the time. This will eventually piss her off more than the mess.

Doghouse Scenario #28 -
Not replacing the empty toilet roll after using it up

The Situation: You spend a good hour in the john, taking in the latest newspaper articles.

You use more than your share of the toilet paper, and as you finish up, you notice the roll is empty. It would be far too much trouble to dig out another roll and attach it, so you decide whoever goes next will get it done!

The Excuse: "Oh, shit! I'm sorry. I thought we were out! I was just going to run to the store and buy more."

Getting Out of the Doghouse: Alright, I'm sure I can reasonably speak for everyone, everywhere when I say that finding the toilet paper roll empty is possibly the most terrible bathroom surprise of all time. (Well, maybe not. Finding pee or other such substances on the floor would probably be worse.) I mean, really, how would you feel if you were constantly having to hobble your way across the bathroom to wherever the extra t.p. is kept, grab a role, hobble back (dribbling all the way) and then attach it.

It takes approximately five seconds to get a new roll when you're done, put it on, and walk away. If you genuinely forget, then apologize, but don't make a big deal out of it, and *don't* do it on purpose.

DOGHOUSE SCENARIO #29 -
Leaving the toilet seat up

The Situation: You're at home, and you feel the need to relieve yourself. It's a pretty normal thing. Upon entering the bathroom, you notice the seat is down. Since you use the head standing 90% of the time (except on special occasions), you do your thing. Then, upon exiting, it never crosses your mind to close the lid. Why should it? You only sit once a day!

The Excuse: "No, really, I was cleaning it."

Getting Out of the Doghouse: Most girls will admit that it's less about courtesy and more about pleasing the eye. If the toilet seat is up, then it's advertising the grime and gross that accumulates there at any given time. It's like a giant germ billboard. And yes, obviously those things are still there when the seat is down, but they're not showing now are they?

Admittedly, it's unpleasant to sit down on the toilet and fall in, having no seat to brace you upright; but, women are far more concerned about someone coming by at random, asking to use the bathroom, and *them* seeing the seat up. And, gentlemen, you should take just as much note of that as women do. The seat is meant to be down honestly. That's why pictures on the front of boxes that encase toilets have the seat depicted that way. It's not because of women— it just looks nicer.

Doghouse Scenario #30 -
Putting off mowing the lawn

The Situation: It's scorching hot outside and you continue to put off mowing the lawn because you're lazy. You procrastinate intentionally, knowing she will eventually get frustrated and do it herself. In addition, she will be mad at you for a solid week, but you reason that she'll get over it.

The Excuse: "But baby, I couldn't resist! You just look so sexy out there sweating and pushing that mower around!"

Getting Out of the Doghouse: We'll give you a hint, guys... a relationship is about teamwork. A balance between everything is absolutely necessary in order to maintain the happiness of all parties. With that said, we understand that sometimes it's tough to be motivated enough to get your share of things done.

Women get that. Sometimes they have trouble too! The important thing to remember is that once you've put it off so many times, even to the point where you're doing it on purpose in the hopes she'll do it, well, that's the point when you are, unfortunately, acting like a child.

The real way to handle this situation is very simple: grow up. Women are, in fact, observant

enough to realize it's hot outside. Also? They are generally most interested in seeing you mow when it's hot. Why? Well, guys, if you're even remotely attractive, we think it's rather obvious. Slip that shirt off, start up the mower, and make it happen. If your lady appreciates the work (and the view) you might even get a tall glass of lemonade and some, uh... "extracurricular activities" for your troubles. Now isn't that worth a little bit of heat and sweat?